A Little Book of

Irish
Sayings

Illustrated by Jon Berkeley

Appletree Press

A man never fails among
his own people.

෪

The person of the greatest talk is
the person of the least work.

CB

Two shorten the road.

ℭ

He who has cattle on the hill
will not sleep easy.

❧

The work praises the man.

One cannot take out of a sack
more than the full of it.

Ȕ

An early riser gets through
his business.

CR

A man lives long in his native place.

ᘓ

It is not a secret if it is known
to three people.

It is better to be alone than
to be in bad company.

The man who won't take advice
will have conflict.

൙

Age is honourable and youth is noble.

CR

It is the quiet pig that eats the meal.

Youth does not mind where it sets foot.

CR

A windy day is not the day
for thatching.

CR

A skill not learned is an enemy.

CB

Everyone lays a burden on
the willing horse.

☙

If there is a hen or a goose,
it will be on the priest's table.

છ

Give the priest his own
side of the road.

❧

Work without end is housewife's work.

❦

There's no bone in the tongue, but
it often broke a man's head.

The fox never found a better
messenger than himself.

CR

There are two sides to every story and
a hundred versions of every song.

∞

It takes time to build castles.

Youth sheds many a skin.

Thirst is the end of drinking and
sorrow is the end of drunkenness.

☙

When the drop is inside
the sense is outside.

❦

A bad egg, a bad bird.

CR

Put silk on a goat and it is still a goat.

You never miss the water
till the well has run dry.

Never bid the devil good morrow
until you meet him.

Live in my heart and pay no rent.

You must live with a person
to know a person.

If you do not sow in spring, you will not reap in autumn.

The well-fed do not
understand the lean.

ᘓ

Woe to him who does not heed
a good wife's counsel.

ႠჁ

The mouth that speaks not
is sweet to hear.

❦

Your feet will bring you to
where your heart is.

Women keep their tongue in their pocket until they marry.

CR

Be good to the child and he will
come to you tomorrow.

CR

A light heart lives long.

She's a good woman, but she didn't take off her boots yet.

Beauty will not make the pot boil.

✂

Choose your company before
you sit down.

CR

A growing moon and a flowing tide
are lucky times to marry in.

❦

It is a lonely washing line that
has no man's shirt on it.

The wearer best knows where
the shoe pinches.

Every man is bold until
he faces a crowd.

ొ

Nobility listens to art.

There is no need like the
lack of a friend.

CR

Needs must when the devil rides.

❦

A gentle answer quenches anger.

ᐲ

Patience is a poultice for all wounds.

॰ॐ॰

Men may meet,
but mountains never greet.

It is a long road that has no turning.

❧

Listen to the sound of the river
and you will catch a trout.

CR

At the beginning and end of your life,
you draw closer to the fire.

First published by
The Appletree Press Ltd
19–21 Alfred Street
Belfast BT2 8DL

Copyright © The Appletree Press Ltd, 1994

A catalogue record for this book is
available from the British Library.

ISBN 0-86281-517-7

9 8 7 6 5 4 3 2 1